Gates of Awe

Texts by:

Robert Orkand
Joyce Orkand
Howard I. Bogot

Illustrated by:

Neil Waldman

Chair, Committee on Children's Liturgy:
Kenneth D. Roseman

The text of the Rosh Hashana Torah reading was adapted by Rabbi Stephen Pearce. The text of the Yom Kippur Torah reading was adapted by Emily Rosenblum.

CCAR Press
Central Conference of American Rabbis
192 Lexington Avenue, New York, NY 10016

Designed by Barry Nostradamus Sher. Composed at Nostradamus Advertising using Xerox Ventura Publisher 2.0 with Professional Extension. English text set in ITC Eras, designed by Albert Beton in collaboration with Albert Hollenstein and digitized by Adobe Systems. Hebrew text set in Lev Yaakov, designed and digitized by Lawrence Kushner. Publisher's Type Foundry was used to re-map Lev Yaakov and create specialized characters.

Library of Congress Cataloging-in-Publication Data

Orkand, Robert
  Gates of awe : texts / by Robert Orkand, Joyce Orkand, Howard I. Bogot : illustrated by Neil Waldman.
      p. cm.
  Summary: Prayers for Rosh Hashanah and Yom Kippur, with appropriate Torah readings.
  ISBN 0-88123-014-6
  1. High Holidays—Liturgy—Texts—Juvenile literature. 2. Reform Judaism—Liturgy—Texts—Juvenile literature. [1. Judaism—Prayer books and devotions. 2. High Holidays.] I. Orkand, Joyce II. Bogot, Howard. III. Waldman, Neil, ill. IV. Title.
296.4'31—dc20   91-7413
                                                      CIP
                                                      AC

Gates of Awe

Holy Day Prayers for Young Children

The publication of this prayerbook is made possible by the
generosity of members of the Westchester Reform Temple
in honor of their beloved rabbi,

Rabbi Jack Stern

Central Conference of American Rabbis

It is important to pray.

בָּרְכוּ אֶת־יְיָ הַמְבֹרָךְ!

Ba-re-chu et A-do-nai
ha-me-vo-rach.

Praise God, to whom our praise is due!

Prayer helps us think about God.

בָּרְכוּ אֶת־יְיָ הַמְבֹרָךְ!

Ba-re-chu et A-do-nai
ha-me-vo-rach.

Praise God, to whom our praise is due!

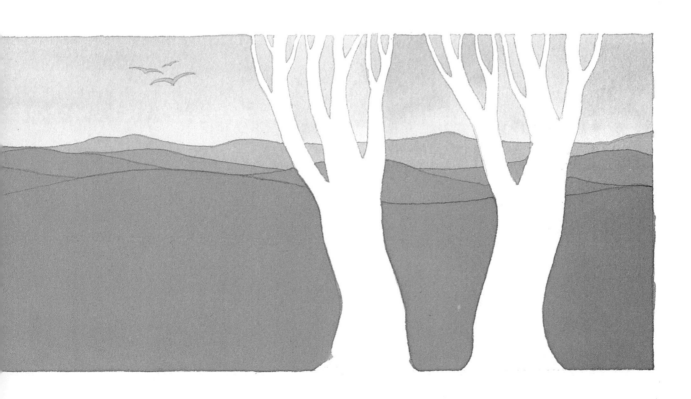

Prayer helps us talk to God.

בָּרְכוּ אֶת־יְיָ הַמְבֹרָךְ!

Ba-re-chu et A-do-nai
ha-me-vo-rach.

Praise God, to whom our praise is due!

Prayer helps us say thank you to God.

בָּרְכוּ אֶת־יְיָ הַמְבֹרָךְ!

בָּרוּךְ יְיָ הַמְבֹרָךְ לְעוֹלָם וָעֶד!

Ba-re-chu et A-do-nai
ha-me-vo-rach.

Ba-ruch A-do-nai ha-me-vo-rach
le-o-lam va-ed.

Praise God, to whom our praise is due!

Praised be God, to whom our praise is due, now and for ever!

When we pray we think about our lives.

People can make a difference.

One me, one you

caring for each other.

One mitzvah helps us

do more mitzvot.

One Torah to study.

One God!

שְׁמַע יִשְׂרָאֵל: יְיָ אֱלֹהֵינוּ, יְיָ אֶחָד!

She-ma Yis-ra-eil: A-do-nai

E-lo-hei-nu, A-do-nai E-chad!

Hear, O Israel: the Eternal is our God,
the Eternal God is One!

בָּרוּךְ שֵׁם כְּבוֹד מַלְכוּתוֹ לְעוֹלָם וָעֶד!

Ba-ruch sheim ke-vod mal-chu-to le-o-lam va-ed!

Blessed is God's glorious rule for ever and ever!

God is always part of the world!

Torah teaches us about God.

וְאָהַבְתָּ אֵת יְיָ אֱלֹהֶיךָ.

Ve-a-hav-ta eit A-do-nai
E-lo-he-cha.

You shall love the Eternal God.

Torah teaches us to love God.

Torah teaches us to think about God.

We think about God when we get up.

We think about God when we go to school.

We think about God when we play.

We think about God when we go to bed.

We think about God.

מִי־כָמְכָה בָּאֵלִם, יְיָ?

מִי כָּמְכָה, נֶאְדָּר בַּקֹדֶשׁ,
נוֹרָא תְהִלֹּת, עֹשֵׂה פֶלֶא?

Mi cha-mo-cha ba-ei-lim,
A-do-nai?

Mi ka-mo-cha, ne-dar

ba-ko-desh, no-ra te-hi-lot, o-sei

fe-leh?

Who is like you, Eternal One, among the gods that are worshipped?

Who is like you, majestic in holiness, awesome in splendor, doing wonders?

Rosh Hashana and Yom Kippur
are days for asking important
questions

and praying for answers.

Who can be like you, O God?

Will the New Year be a happy
one for all people?

אָבִינוּ מַלְכֵּנוּ.

A-vi-nu Mal-kei-nu.

Like a mother, like a father,

God acts in special ways.

אָבִינוּ מַלְכֵּנוּ.

A-vi-nu Mal-kei-nu.

God helped Jews who lived
long ago.

אָבִינוּ מַלְכֵּנוּ.

A-vi-nu Mal-kei-nu.

God hears our prayers today.

אָבִינוּ מַלְכֵּנוּ.

A-vi-nu Mal-kei-nu.

God helps us to make tomorrow safe.

אָבִינוּ מַלְכֵּנוּ.

A-vi-nu Mal-kei-nu.

Like a mother, like a father

God acts in special ways.

Reading of the Torah

Stand and open Ark

We are the Jewish people.

We have a treasure.

Our treasure is the Torah.

In it we read the stories of Jews who lived long ago:

Abraham, Isaac, and Jacob;

Sarah, Rebekah, Leah, and Rachel.

In it are words that teach us how to be kinder, friendlier and more helpful.

In it are words that teach us how to celebrate Shabbat and the Holy Days.

In Torah are words that speak of our love of God.

Take Torah from Ark

This is our Torah.

Its words speak of hope, of love,
of truth and of goodness.

This is the Torah.

הָבוּ גֹדֶל לֵאלֹהֵינוּ
וּתְנוּ כָבוֹד לַתּוֹרָה.

Ha-vu go-del lei-lo-hei-nu
u-te-nu cha-vod la-To-rah.

Let us declare the greatness of our God
and give honor to the Torah.

כִּי מִצִּיּוֹן תֵּצֵא תוֹרָה,
וּדְבַר־יְיָ מִירוּשָׁלָיִם.

Ki mi-tsi-yon tei-tsei To-rah

u-de-var A-do-nai

mi-ru-sha-la-yim.

For out of Zion shall go forth Torah,
and the word of God from Jerusalem.

בָּרְכוּ אֶת־יְיָ הַמְבֹרָךְ!

בָּרוּךְ יְיָ הַמְבֹרָךְ לְעוֹלָם וָעֶד!

בָּרוּךְ אַתָּה, יְיָ אֱלֹהֵינוּ, מֶלֶךְ הָעוֹלָם, אֲשֶׁר בָּחַר־בָּנוּ מִכָּל־הָעַמִּים וְנָתַן־לָנוּ אֶת־תּוֹרָתוֹ. בָּרוּךְ אַתָּה, יְיָ, נוֹתֵן הַתּוֹרָה.

Ba-re-chu et A-do-nai
ha-me-vo-rach!

Ba-ruch A-do-nai ha-me-vo-rach
le-o-lam va-ed!

בָּרְכוּ אֶת יְיָ הַמְבֹרָךְ

Ba-ruch a-ta, A-do-nai
E-lo-hei-nu, me-lech ha-o-lam,
a-sher ba-char ba-nu mi-kol
ha-a-mim, ve-na-tan la-nu et
To-ra-to. Ba-ruch a-ta, A-do-nai,
no-tein ha-To-rah.

Praise the Eternal One, to whom our praise is due!

Praised be the Eternal One, to whom our praise is due, now and for ever!

Praised be the Eternal God, Ruler of time and space. You have called us to serve You by giving us Your Torah. Praised be the Eternal God, Giver of the Torah.

Abraham is known as the father of the Jewish people.

Abraham is also called the first Jew.

Abraham loved and trusted God.

Isaac was Abraham and Sarah's most beloved son.

Isaac was born when they were both very old.

27

28

Abraham's neighbors often sacrificed their children to their many gods.

But Abraham knew that these gods were not really God. They were false gods.

Adonai was the true God.

Adonai created heaven and earth.

Abraham was sure that his God was not the kind of God who wanted the death of a child.

Still, God wished to test Abraham.

God asked Abraham to go to a far-off place that was hard to find.

There God asked Abraham to sacrifice his son, Isaac, his only, special son.

Abraham went to that place because he knew that God would protect Isaac.

When Abraham and Isaac reached that secret place,

God said: "I will not hurt your son.

"I wanted to be sure that you would listen to My voice.

"I know that you believe in me.

"Now I will bless you.

"You will be an example to other people.

"Your children will be known in all the world.

"And they will remember your courage and trust."

34

Abraham looked toward heaven.

He thanked God.

He took Isaac by the hand,

returned home,

and every year spoke of his meeting with God.

Continue with Torah Blessings on page 44

Our Torah tells us that God sent messages to the Jewish people.

Moses was God's very special messenger.

Moses was a most important Jewish teacher because he taught us lessons from God.

God told Moses to tell us to act in special ways,

to love our parents,

to care for strangers,

to care for those poorer than ourselves,

and to share with strangers.

God told Moses to tell the Jewish people not to steal,

not to lie,

to be fair,

to try and understand how others feel,

to love our families,

to respect older people,

and to be honest.

God told Moses to tell us to care about people with special needs,

to speak loudly and clearly when people have trouble hearing,

to walk with those who cannot run,

to talk about beauty to those who have trouble seeing.

God told Moses to tell us

to love ourselves,

to love the world,

and to love God, the only God.

בָּרוּךְ אַתָּה, יְיָ אֱלֹהֵינוּ, מֶלֶךְ
הָעוֹלָם, אֲשֶׁר נָתַן לָנוּ תּוֹרַת
אֱמֶת וְחַיֵּי עוֹלָם נָטַע בְּתוֹכֵנוּ.

בָּרוּךְ אַתָּה, יְיָ, נוֹתֵן הַתּוֹרָה.

Ba-ruch a-ta, A-do-nai

E-lo-hei-nu, me-lech ha-o-lam,

a-sher na-tan la-nu To-rat e-met,

ve-cha-yei o-lam na-ta

be-to-chei-nu.

Ba-ruch a-ta, A-do-nai, no-tein

ha-To-rah.

Praised be the Eternal God, Ruler of time and space, who has given us a Torah of truth, implanting within us eternal life.

Praised be the Eternal God, Giver of the Torah.

On Rosh Hashana continue here.
On Yom Kippur, go to page 48

Shofar sounds remind us to listen to the words of people we love.

Shofar sounds tell us it's time to pray.

Shofar sounds help us pay attention to the important lessons in Torah.

We hear the shofar on Rosh Hashana.

Listen to the sounds of the shofar:

בָּרוּךְ אַתָּה, יְיָ אֱלֹהֵינוּ, מֶלֶךְ הָעוֹלָם, אֲשֶׁר קִדְּשָׁנוּ בְּמִצְוֹתָיו וְצִוָּנוּ לִשְׁמֹעַ קוֹל שׁוֹפָר.

Ba-ruch a-ta, A-do-nai

E-lo-hei-nu, me-lech ha-o-lam,

a-sher ki-de-sha-nu be-mits-vo-tav

ve-tsi-va-nu lish-mo-a kol sho-far.

Blessed is the Eternal our God, Ruler of the universe, who hallows us with Mitzvot, and calls us to hear the sound of the shofar.

Teki-a...Shevarim...Teru-a...Teki-a.

The Torah teaches us

to think about God,

to remember the Sabbath day
and make it special,

to honor our parents,

to love our neighbors as
ourselves,

to study Torah,

and to love Torah.

הוֹדוֹ עַל אֶרֶץ וְשָׁמָיִם,
וַיָּרֶם קֶרֶן לְעַמּוֹ, תְּהִלָּה
לְכָל־חֲסִידָיו, לִבְנֵי
יִשְׂרָאֵל עַם קְרוֹבוֹ.
הַלְלוּיָהּ.

Ho-do al e-rets ve-sha-ma-yim,

ve-ya-rem ke-ren le-a-mo, te-hi-la

le-chol cha-si-dav, li-ve-nei

Yis-ra-eil, am ke-ro-vo.

Ha-le-lu-yah!

Your splendor covers heaven and earth;

You give strength to your people; faithful Israel glories in You. Halleluyah!

In the Torah are words that speak of God.

Its words teach us how to live.

We will study Torah.

We will love Torah.

עֵץ־חַיִּים הִיא לַמַּחֲזִיקִים
בָּהּ, וְתֹמְכֶיהָ מְאֻשָּׁר.
דְּרָכֶיהָ דַרְכֵי־נֹעַם,
וְכָל־נְתִיבוֹתֶיהָ שָׁלוֹם.

Eits cha-yim hi la-ma-cha-zi-kim
ba, ve-to-me-che-ha me-u-shar.
De-ra-che-ha da-re-chei no-am,
ve-chol ne-ti-vo-te-ha sha-lom.

It is a tree of life to those who hold it fast, and all who cling to it find happiness. Its ways are ways of pleasantness, and all its paths are peace.

Continue here on Rosh Hashana
On Yom Kippur, go to page 57

Rosh Hashana is the birthday of the world.

As the world grows older, we grow older, too.

As we grow older, we will try to make the world better.

We will try to protect animals.

We will try to plant flowers.

We will try to care for the place in which we live.

We will try to make the world quiet and peaceful.

O God, help us be happier today than yesterday.

O God, help me act more bravely tomorrow than I acted today.

O God, help me tell others about the shofar.

We hear the shofar sound on Rosh Hashana and Yom Kippur.

Listen to the sounds of the shofar:

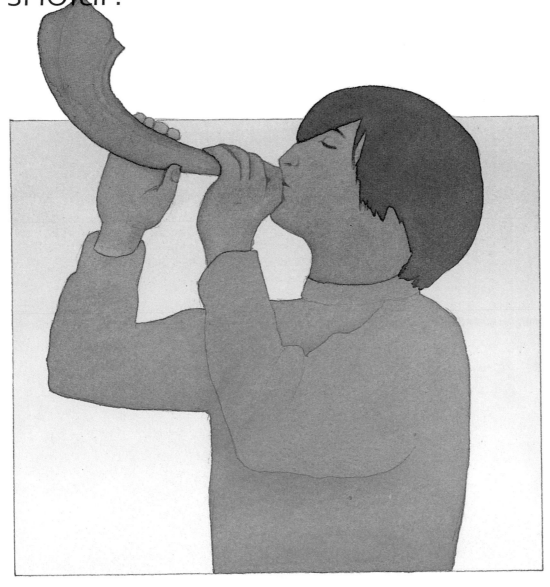

בָּרוּךְ אַתָּה, יְיָ אֱלֹהֵינוּ, מֶלֶךְ הָעוֹלָם, אֲשֶׁר קִדְּשָׁנוּ בְּמִצְוֹתָיו וְצִוָּנוּ לִשְׁמֹעַ קוֹל שׁוֹפָר.

Ba-ruch a-ta, A-do-nai

E-lo-hei-nu, me-lech ha-o-lam,

a-sher ki-de-sha-nu

be-mits-vo-tav, ve-tsi-va-nu

lish-mo-a kol sho-far.

Blessed is the Eternal our God, Ruler of the universe, who hallows us with Mitzvot, and calls us to hear the sound of the shofar.

Teki-a...Shevarim...Teru-a...Teki-a Gedola

On Rosh Hashana, end here

Yom Kippur is a special time for saying
"I'm sorry."

We are sorry for not sharing.

We are sorry for not being gentle.

We are sorry for not telling the truth.

We are sorry for not being helpful.

For all these things, we say "I'm sorry" to our families.

We say "I'm sorry" to our teachers, friends, and neighbors.

We say "I'm sorry" to God.

Yom Kippur reminds us

to be kind,

to share,

to be gentle,

to tell the truth,

to be helpful,

to be happy,

to think about yesterday, today,
and tomorrow.

O God, help us be happier today than yesterday.

O God, help me act more bravely tomorrow than I acted today.

O God, help me tell others about the shofar.

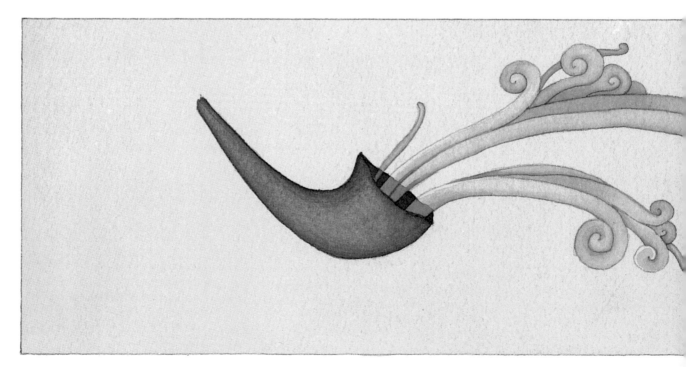

We hear the shofar sound on Rosh Hashana and Yom Kippur.

Listen to the sounds of the shofar:

בָּרוּךְ אַתָּה, יְיָ אֱלֹהֵינוּ, מֶלֶךְ הָעוֹלָם, אֲשֶׁר קִדְּשָׁנוּ בְּמִצְוֹתָיו וְצִוָּנוּ לִשְׁמוֹעַ קוֹל שׁוֹפָר.

Ba-ruch a-ta, A-do-nai

E-lo-hei-nu, me-lech ha-o-lam,

a-sher ki-de-sha-nu

be-mits-vo-tav, ve-tsi-va-nu

lish-mo-a kol sho-far.

Blessed is the Eternal our God, Ruler of the universe, who hallows us with Mitzvot, and calls us to hear the sound of the shofar.

Teki-a...Shevarim...Teru-a...Teki-a Gedola

On Yom Kippur, end here